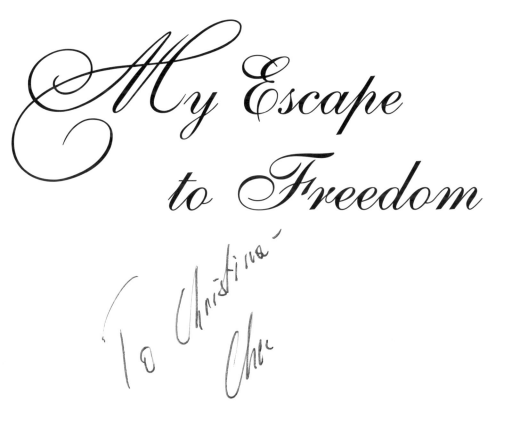

My Escape to Freedom

To Christina
Chez

Poems & Reflections

Chez Raginiak

Library of Congress Control Number: 2008905180

ISBN: 9780982507100

Printed in China

Published by
1Moment, LLC
P.O. Box 5555
Hopkins, MN 55343 USA

www.1moment.us

I dedicate this book to my children,
Monika and Ania.
Dream great dreams, girls.

Turn your wounds into wisdom.

Oprah Winfrey

THANK YOU

Friends and relatives risked their freedom to help me escape from communist Poland. Strangers became my friends in the refugee camp. Wonderful people in Clarion, Iowa, helped me start life in America. And now, I thank those whose help was a gift in completing this book: Monika, Maciej, and Piotr Raginiak, Sandy Ryan, Marly Cornell, Janet Fuchek, Rachel Arntson, Bob and Adrienne Hastings, Kara Johnson, Robin Medrud, and many others.

A special thank you to Betty Liedtke, whose vision, faith, and talent helped me put this book together, and to Janie Jasin, whose compassion, confidence, and enthusiasm helped me bring it out into the world.

Thank you all. Without your support I would not have become who I am today or the person I wish to become tomorrow.

INTRODUCTION

$\mathcal{O}$ver a period of years, I put my immigrant story into songs and short stories. I even started writing a memoir. Then, I looked again at the numerous poems I had written during the same time, and I realized the poems told my story.

After putting these poems together and reading them several times, it occurred to me that they don't just tell my story—of an immigrant coming to America—they tell the story of every person in every nation. They tell about escapes to all types of freedom: freedom to do what we choose and to express our thoughts, feelings, and emotions; freedom from the memories of our tumultuous pasts, from dependencies on others, and from the fears, paradigms, habits, and addictions that can end our lives and destroy those whom we love; and freedom from being afraid to live the life we were born to live.

Escape often seems to be the only way out to freedom—as it was in my case in communist Poland. Finding strength for such decisions is crucial. Seeing how we succeeded in the past can help us with future problems—and can lead us to the type of life where no escape is necessary: a fulfilling life, a life where the first thing we see in the mirror each morning is a smile.

To help you become more aware of meaningful moments, life-altering events, and special people who made a difference in your life's path, I invite you to reflect on your life and appreciate the friendships and relationships you have created. Be proud for the mountains you have scaled and the peaks you have reached thus far, and for the oceans you have already crossed to achieve your dreams and desires.

Several of the poems may be more easily understood with an explanation of the circumstances they encompass. For that reason, a brief background reflection is included at the end of each chapter.

It is my great privilege to share my experiences with you.

CONTENTS

CHAPTER I

Living Under Communism

Our lives teach us who we are.

Salman Rushdie

LOOKING FOR MY FATHER

*D*o you remember that night in March, Mama,
The ugliest month in our country, when we went looking for a drunk daddy?
Yes, I remember, kiddo, but I wish you would forget it.
Why do you hang on to those rotten memories, child?
I try not to, but they sit in my mind,
In some dark family drawer there.
That drawer has all the bad stuff, Mama.

That night, we walked to the tiny town where he worked and drank.
I heard you crying most of the way.
To see our path, we looked to the sky.
The stars shining between the two rows of trees showed our feet where to go.
After a three-mile walk, we finally arrived in that God-forsaken village
With only one streetlight beaming in the darkness
Like a lighthouse to the sea.
We checked Daddy's office. We checked around the locked tavern.
No sign of him. No sign of anyone.

And then rain came.

The whole town was in a deep sleep. Only we were awake, very awake.
Do you know what, Mama? I felt like I lost my father that night. I think I did.
I thought he and every living creature in this town left us,
As if only the two of us were alive in my cold, twelve-year-old world.

I was ready to walk home; but you, Mama, you did not quit.
You didn't stop looking for him. But then, how could you?
You walked around some warehouse,
Looked behind each toothless fence while I stood under the streetlight.
Sometimes from the left side, sometimes from the right,
I heard you calling Daddy's name.

I will never forget that night, Mama. How could I?
I was cold and wet.
Water ran down my back, down to my already soaked feet.
Then my tears, mixed with the raindrops, trickled down my cheeks,
Dripped down my chin, my chest,
To land on the ground and mix with the muddy rainwater flowing by my feet
Like a river of fear and tears.

A kingdom founded on injustice never lasts.

Seneca

THE REFRIGERATOR

*T*he milk goes sour after hours of sitting in a warm hallway.
Flies sit on the edge of the milk can like crows on a power line
Marking their turf with black dots of boredom and disrespect.
The smell keeps even our thirstiest cat away.

We need a refrigerator more than we needed heat.
Six children squeal for dinner like birds in a nest.
Preserving the food we have is as important as gathering it in the first place,
So that none of us go to bed hungry or sick.

At a milkless dinner, a decision is made to start saving money,
To sell flowers and vegetables at the corner of Lenin Street,
Empty every piggy bank, look under each worn-out sofa,
Collect all we can to buy our first-ever fridge.

By sunrise, sixth in line outside the store, I join the crowd of shoppers.
Names are taken, and the list of buyers is closed.
Blankets are spread, folding chairs open,
Weeks of waiting are ahead of us.

Every few days we're told the truck is coming,
That refrigerators will come for the dozens who wait.
But fourteen hot days and nights later
Only five small, red refrigerators arrive.

*Nothing is politically right
which is morally wrong.*

Daniel O'Connell

MARTIAL LAW

It was the coldest Sunday morning of my life:
December 13th, 1981.
Everything froze overnight:
Lakes,
Rivers,
The Baltic Sea,
Radios,
Televisions,
Telephones,
Buses,
Trains,
Airplanes,
Schools,
Shops,
Factories,
Small towns,
Large cities.
The whole nation froze.
Nothing moved.
No one could talk.

Martial law had begun.

Reflection

For the youngest of six children, life wasn't easy in the '60s and '70s in communist Poland. During my childhood, I did not understand any of the Cold War politics and dynamics. All I knew was that with my older siblings out of the house, I had to help my mother deal with an alcoholic father and brother. From age ten until I left Poland at age twenty-five, I lived with the constant fear of either of them coming home at any hour, drunk and furious, and starting a fight with anybody, for any reason. I trained myself to wake up in the night to the slightest noise.

In addition to family problems, my life in Poland was becoming more unbearable by the end of the '70s and the early '80s due to the failing political system.

After martial law started on December 13, 1981, rationing began. With special tickets (or coupons), my family could buy 2 kilos of sugar, 2.5 kilos of meat, and 1 bottle of vodka per adult, per month, in addition to other miscellaneous items. Many people drowned their despair in alcohol in those days, despite limited supplies.

My father, an amateur poet and would-be Catholic priest (his personal plans changed after he met my mother), started his career as the vice-mayor in my hometown, Lukta, right after World War II. However, due to our anti-communist family history (during 1942-43, three of my uncles joined the Home Army, loyal to the Polish government in exile, which was seen by Stalin as an obstacle to his socialist plans for Eastern Europe), my father was demoted over time to a co-op vice president. Thirty years later, he ended up at the bottom of his professional path, working as a night watchman. He died in 1989. The circumstances of his death remain unknown.

We know now that declaring martial law was perhaps the best option the Polish leader, General Wojciech Jaruzelski, had in order to prevent the Soviet Army from occupying Poland. Under martial law, the government was able to control all aspects of our country's life and infrastructure, from the media, communication and transportation, to employment and food supplies. Only then could they try to stop or reduce the spread of freedom inspired by the workers' union, Solidarity, led by Lech Walesa. The movement, in concert with other factors, was the beginning of the end for the Warsaw Pact and, eventually, the Soviet Union.

CHAPTER II

Leaving Poland

The only way to predict the future is to have power to shape the future.

Eric Hoffer

SEEKING STRENGTH: PART I

I look into my baby mirror.
I see dark hair,
Squinty eyes,
Six candles on my birthday cake.

I look closer.
I touch it to my nose.
I spill my breath on it.
My reflection disappears in the fog.

Slowly, my sleeve brings me back into view.
First my left cheek.
I see a scar,
I see myself in the future.
Should I peek more?
Do I want to know what will become of me?
I'm scared.
I'm still a baby.
I cry, and my tears fall on the mirror.
They splash quietly and wash off the fog.

One teardrop falls off the top of the glass.
I see white hair on my head,
I see an old man.

Another tear falls at the bottom,
Uncovering my wrinkled hands.

My last tear falls right in the middle
And flows down my chest
Like a raindrop on a dusty window.
I can see through the streak
That my heart—my heart—is made of stone.

There is no lasting hope in violence,
only temporary relief from hopelessness.

Kingman Brewster, Jr.

THEY BEAT HOPE OUT OF US

A bus stop, not even a station,
Just a three-wall hut with a cheap plastic roof
And three benches fastened to a cracked cement floor,
Our hangout on Saturday nights.

Soon after we gathered, everyone in town could hear our voices,
Laugh at our anarchist jokes,
Relate to our lives—lives with no choices.

And then they came.
To silence our mouths,
To kill our optimism,
To root out any desire for change in us.
With their fast-swinging arms
And bone-crushing batons,
They showered our innocent legs, backs, and heads
With their own disappointments,
Ignorance,
Fake superiority,
Brains poisoned by communist dogma.

A bus stop, not even a station,
Just a three-wall hut with a cheap plastic roof
And three benches fastened to a cracked cement floor,
A perfect place to beat hope out of us.

The next day,
Not even the stains of our blood on the bus stop floor,
Or echoes of our laments within the walls,
Stopped life from creeping forward,
As if nothing had happened.

*You need chaos in your soul
to give birth to a dancing star.*

Friedrich Nietzsche

SEEKING STRENGTH: PART II

*M*y mirror is missing.
They took it away.
No matter how hard I look,
I can never find it.
I don't know how I look anymore,
Who I am anymore.

I've run through woods for 25 years, looking for my mirror,
But all I've found is a lake on the edge of the forest.
I kneel by its shore every day now and bow over the water.
This is the only place in my world where I have an identity.
I recognize my dark hair and squinty eyes.
I remember that boy!

I pick up the lake and carry it home.
I shout to people, "I found my self and you can, too!"
But they don't listen.
They don't believe it can be done.

I hide the lake in my pocket and walk westward
Where, I hear, all the people have mirrors.
I pick up the pace, faster and faster.
I run.
I run away.

*A mother understands
what a child does not say.*

Jewish Proverb

GOODBYE

*P*acked and ready to leave,
I stepped outside.
Preoccupied with peeling potatoes by the front door,
She kept her eyes from me.

What do I tell her?

This is the last time we see each other, Mama.
I, I made up my mind.
I planned all this secretly for years.
All I have left to do is to climb on the bus and wave goodbye.

She grabbed another potato,
Glanced at me for a moment,
Almost said something.

But you will come back, won't you, Son?
These lakes and forests can't live without you.
We can't live without you.
And who will eat these potatoes?

How many times did I see her in this position?
Cleaning mushrooms I found, or fish I caught?

Her shaking hands stopped peeling for a moment.
What do I tell these woods and waters when they ask for you?
What do I tell your guitars when dust and rust overwhelm them,
When they miss the touch of your hands?
What do I tell my hands when they miss the squeeze of yours?
What do I tell? What do I tell, Son?

I looked at her.
Oh, Mama!
And my tears said what my lips could not.
She answered with her tears falling on the potatoes.
In silence, we cried out our goodbye.

Reflection

*T*he decision to leave my homeland was the most difficult I ever had to make. I had to be careful not to tell anyone about my plans. Having limited information about where refugee camps were in Europe, I assumed there was only one, in Traiskirchen, Austria. In preparation for entering Traiskirchen, I took private classes in German, the official language of Austria.

At that time Polish officials did not issue passports to ordinary citizens who wanted to visit any of the western nations. They feared—rightly so—that travelers would not return. However, the government could not prevent us from wanting to see the Holy Father (the Polish Pope) in Italy, since 95 percent of Poles were Catholics. That was my route of escape—to purchase a bus ticket to Italy and convince the authorities that I intended to return.

I needed two years' wages to pay for my ticket. Coming up with such an amount at one time was beyond hope. Fortunately, someone I trusted lent me that enormous sum, two hundred dollars, so I could leave. His name was Andrzej Peplowski.

Hopelessness is the word that comes to mind most when I look back on my life in Poland. Before I left, I shared a ten by fourteen-foot room with a roommate. Six guys rented three rooms next to each other in the basement of a house. We shared one bathroom with no hot water or shower, and to take a shower in the upstairs bathroom (only one per week) we had to arrange it with the landlord. I had no money and no better job in sight. That was it for me, and I could no longer accept such a life.

Saying goodbye to my friends was hard. Some of them knew about my plans. The others found out when, about two weeks later, the local newspaper announced, "One of the tourists vanished on the streets of Italy and never returned." However, saying goodbye to my mother was much harder. I was not sure if I would be forced to stay or, if I left, if I would be forced to re-turn. There was still a chance that the Polish Secret Service might have pre-vented me from leaving, so I did not want to worry her prematurely. She would have agonized for ten days, just to see me return. So I did not say anything. Still, she felt something was about to happen. She asked me the day before I left if I was coming back. I could only answer her with my tears; she could only do the same.

CHAPTER III

Austria

*In the middle of every
difficulty lies opportunity.*

Albert Einstein

WHERE I BECAME A MAN

*K*icked out of five police stations,
Told to go back,
Trembling, I sit on an empty bench in downtown Vienna.

It was not supposed to be this way!
I crossed the mountains on foot for nothing?
Going back to Italy with no money is impossible.
Returning to Poland means jail.
I stay.

I sit on a bench in downtown Vienna,
Where cars rush by,
Where people walk by,
Where lives pass by,
Almost touchable,
But unstoppable,
And only I am motionless at the greatest crossroads of my life.

What's next?
Where should I go,
With no money,
No language,
No map,
No ideas?

I am sitting on a bench in downtown Vienna,
Hungry,
Thirsty,
Dirty,
Lost.

That is where I became a man.

"Come to the edge," he said.
They said, "We are afraid."
"Come to the edge," he said.
They came. He pushed them...
and they flew.

Guillaume Apollinaire

THE REFUGEE CAMP

Welcome to the refugee camp in Traiskirchen, Austria,
A place where dreams start and end,
Where lives are decided,
Where people are numbers.

Welcome to the first stop to freedom, refugees,
A place that can give you wings or break your legs,
Where people start believing in God,
Where they turn to the devil for help.

Welcome to the last stop close to your homeland, immigrants,
A place where you can still turn around and walk home,
Where people don't care if you do,
Where only the young and healthy move on.

Welcome to your temporary home, all who escaped the old one,
A place where all languages are spoken,
Where doors can be broken at two in the morning,
Where you can be killed for a bottle of booze.

Welcome to the school of life, brave souls,
A place where characters are made or destroyed,
Where street smarts prevail,
Where you'll see your countrymen sleeping in potholes.

Welcome to what we have chosen, we, the future of new nations.
There is no easy way to start a new life,
A life worth the sacrifices we made,
A life better than the one we risked.

*Strength does not come
from physical capacity.
It comes from an indomitable will.*

Mahatma Gandhi

STOJKA*

I am standing by the curb of "Refugee Street,"
Just outside the refugee camp,
Right next to a sign: "Working outside the camp is prohibited!"

I am not alone.
There are hundreds of us here,
Poles, Russians, Hungarians, Albanians,
All mixed like hay in a stack,
All waving with hands of hope,
To be chosen to work,
To slave,
On our road to freedom.

Oh, yes, I learned all the right answers in German:
Can I pick weeds? "I am a weed killer!"
Can I take care of horses? "I was born on one!"
Can I lay bricks? "I used to build pyramids!"

I need work!

I need money to help my family back home,
To buy food and clothes for me here
Or a bar of chocolate for my sweets-deprived mouth,
To feel like a human,
Like you, people of Austria.

But, like an unpopular prostitute,
I am chosen by no one.

* Polish for standing by the side of a road hoping to be chosen for work.

Yesterday I dared to struggle.
Today I dare to win.

Bernadette Devlin

LUCKY MAN

After each day of illegal work outside the camp,
We rush to the announcement board located by the gate
To check if we are selected to fly away.

With dirty fingers and eager eyes
We follow down the names on the list behind the glass.
Sometimes we hear, "I am going to Canada!"
Sometimes, "Australia!"
But most often we hear, "Not yet."
I wait.

The rainy summer dries out.
The colorful autumn fades.
The Austrian winter is coming,
When we enter the camp for the hundredth time
And, as usual, walk to the board,
Follow the names on the list
And hear another "Hurray!"
But this time, finally,
The cheer is mine!

Right there, by the gate,
I ask the guard to polka with me.
Then I dance with a cook and a janitor.
Oh! What a dance of relief it is!
Then I kiss the board
And rush to my friends to share the news.

Later,
There are bottles of cheap champagne,
Tears of joy,
Hugs of finality,
Phone calls of goodbye,
And fears of the unknown.

Oh, yes!
I am a lucky man.
I am going to America.

Reflection

$\mathscr{B}$ecause I did not ask anyone for the location of refugee camps in Europe, I did not know there was one in Italy where I could have gone. Instead, I focused my energy and limited resources (a can of tuna, two slices of bread, and about $25) on crossing the border between Italy and Austria and finding the refugee camp in Austria.

From Venice, I traveled by bus to Udine, a large town in northeastern Italy. I headed for the nearest border crossing between the two countries. From Udine, by train, I went to a small town, Tarvisio, next to the border. There, I could see mountains ahead of me. I crossed them on foot and went around the border crossing. I was finally in Austria, where I could use my broken German and spend the rest of my money on a train ticket to the capital city.

In Vienna, tired and hungry but excited, I bravely marched to the first police station I found to turn myself in. Surprisingly, when I told them who I was and how I got there, they opened the door, yelled at me, and pushed me out. The same thing happened several more times until I understood that I should not have crossed the border illegally. I could have been arrested and deported to Poland. There was a refugee camp near Rome I should have gone to. Desperate, I wandered the streets of Vienna. In the evening, I drifted to the hallways of the main train station where I found a kiosk with people helping immigrants. They gave me a few shillings, bought me a ticket, and sent me to a town where the camp was located—Traiskirchen. I arrived after the gates were closed. That night I slept on a park bench and entered the camp in the morning.

After entering the camp, we refugees were isolated for about a week while a background check was run on us, basic medical tests were performed, and our stories were written down. If all went well, we were given bedding and sent to one of the rooms we shared with ten or more others. Then, the waiting started.

Prior to 1985, each refugee had several countries to choose from. By the middle of 1985 only three nations were accepting immigrants from Poland: Australia, Canada, and the USA. Each choice required moving to another continent.

Depending on the new country's needs and immigrant quota, some people spent months in the camp, some years, and some never left Austria if they were too old or sick, or did not have strong enough reasons to receive asylum. The least fortunate eventually had to return home and face prosecution, ridicule, or poverty.

Looking for an illegal job in Traiskirchen was a process repeated for as long as the camp had been in existence. Officially, we were not allowed to work outside the camp but, in reality, most of us did. The pay was low, the shifts were long, and the treatment was often heartless. Nevertheless, we accepted any job offered from local farmers or construction companies. We needed money. And we needed to stay busy to stay sane.

The most joyful day in any immigrant's life is the day we learn the date of departure to our final destination. In my case, it was the United States of America. My day was December 10, 1985. Destination: Des Moines, Iowa. As it turned out, the final destination was Clarion, Iowa, located a one-and-a-half-hour drive north from the state's capital.

CHAPTER IV

America

PART ONE: Coming To America

*Life's challenges are
not supposed to paralyze you,
they're supposed to help you
discover who you are.*

Bernice Johnson Reagon

WELCOME TO AMERICA

Welcome to America,
To your home,
The land of the high sky, where dreams and eagles fly.

Welcome to America,
Where wide, never-ending roads
Take us to desired destinations,
Where we can be all we can.

Welcome to America,
The melting pot of people,
The vegetable salad of races,
The deep forest of cultures,
The burning jungle of issues.

Welcome to America,
To sleepless cities,
Silent canyons,
Helpful neighbors.

Welcome to America,
To your home,
My home now, too,
The land of the high sky, where dreams and eagles fly.

There is more hunger
for love and appreciation
in this world than for bread.

Mother Teresa of Calcutta

THANKFUL

"Hello, my name is Chez Raginiak.
I speak no English. Help!"
That was my English vocabulary as of December 11, 1985,
When I arrived at five after midnight in frigid Iowa.

But, so what that I wore tennis shoes and a sweater when I arrived
In 10 below and there was no one to meet me at the airport?

So what that nobody in Clarion spoke my native language,
And there was no job for me?

So what that when I found one I had to work one week
For free to prove myself?

So what that I waited days for a telephone connection
To tell my family that I was okay?

So what that I couldn't find English sounds in my mouth,
And I was the subject of ethnic jokes?

So what that I worked as a stock boy,
And I biked to work in the snowy winter?

So what that my beginnings were hard?

I was thankful I had clothes when I was cold,
Food when I was hungry,
Music when I wanted to sing,
Books when I wanted to read,
A church when I needed to pray,
Friends when I needed someone to be close
So, if only for a moment,
I could feel like a normal person again.

I never wanted to go away,
and the hard part now
is the leaving you all.
I'm not afraid, but it seems
as if I should be homesick
for you even in heaven.

Louisa May Alcott

HOMESICK

*I*t made my love greater,
Mother older,
Father shorter,
Siblings closer,
Friends dearer.

It made my steps slower,
Walks farther,
Smiles invisible,
Trembling of hands uncontrollable.

It made my chest tight,
Lungs small,
Breaths shallow,
Pillows wet.

It made my hair gray,
Ears deaf,
Eyes sad.

It made my handwriting faster,
Phone calls longer,
Feelings truer,
Nights darker.

It made my meals tasteless,
Guitar distant,
Speeches silent,
Dreams doubtful.

It made my prayers, prayers.

*The happiest of all lives
is a busy solitude.*

Voltaire

SHOCK

Imagining life in America:

1. Save some money.
2. Own a house.
3. Get a car.
4. Buy insurance.
5. Have fun shopping.
6. Invest for old age.
7. Enjoy life!

Living life in America:

One: Savings Account, Money Market Account, Certificate of Deposit, Savings Bonds, Short-term, Long-term, and Notice Accounts…

Two: FHA, VA, Jumbo, Balloon, Option ARM, Fixed-rate ARM, Two-Step Mortgage, Buydown, Conventional…

Three: 4-Door Sedans, 2-Door Coupes, Station Wagons, Convertibles, Mini-Vans, SUVs, Pickup Trucks, Hybrids…

Four: Personal Accident and Illness, Income Protection, Trauma, Term Life, Whole Life, Fire and Theft…

Five: Retail, Department, Mail-order, Men's Wear, Women's Apparel, Farm Equipment, Liquor Stores, Hardware…

Six: IRC 401k, IRC 403b, Annuities, 457, Pension Plans, SIMPLE IRAs, Profit-Sharing Plans…

Seven: When???

*When we long for life
without difficulties, remind us that
oaks grow strong in contrary winds and
diamonds are made under pressure.*

Peter Marshall

SHOPPING FOR MY FIRST MIRROR

The day finally came;
We were going to a store to shop for my first mirror.

On the main floor there were mirrors of all sizes and needs.
The left wall was covered with round mirrors of satisfaction.
The right wall was plastered with square mirrors of individuality.
The second floor was filled with large-sized mirrors of haves:
Big homes, large lots, large cars, large hearts.

I never knew there could be so many mirrors!
And they were all different!

Carefully, I placed several mirrors in my shopping cart
And took them to a fitting room.
I put on one of happiness,
But it didn't fit.
I tried to force on a mirror of love,
But they did not have my size that day.

I begged the store clerk, "Any hope of finding one for me?"

They had a sale that day
On mirrors of work and possibility,
Adjustment and appreciation,
A new language and culture,
A new life and new home.

They were two-for-one;
I bought them all.

On my way out, from the corner of my eye,
I saw a tiny mirror by the window, shining in the sun.
I asked if I could try it on.
And I did.
It fit.
I bought it,
My first-ever mirror of hope.

*The limits of my language
mean the limits of my world.*

Ludwig Wittgenstein

I NEED TO LEARN THE LANGUAGE

I need to learn the language,
So I can tell about my pain,
About my fears,
My desires.
So I can sing with my children,
Guide them,
Pray.

I need to learn the language,
So I can understand the whisper of my destiny,
Follow it,
Fulfill it.

I need to learn the language,
So I can travel the future
With no misunderstood goals,
No mispronounced intentions.

I need to learn the language,
So I can live.

*Destiny is not a matter of chance;
it is a matter of choice.
It is not a thing to be waited for;
it is a thing to be achieved.*

W. J. Bryant

THIS IS THE HOME I CREATED

A large house in the suburbs
On one acre of hilly land,
With a swimming pool and a volleyball court,
Two cars, a boat,
Two kids and a cat.
Perfect!
I'm proud. So proud.

On weekends, I go to our land by the lake.
There is no city noise there.
No rush to get things done,
No traffic,
TV,
Phones,
People.
Only the lake, the trees,
And the birds.
Peaceful. So peaceful.

The smell of the woods,
The hum of the wind,
The splash of the fish,
Effortless. So effortless.

This is the home I created.

*Some memories are realities,
and are better than anything that can
ever happen to one again.*

Willa Cather

OUR VIDEO CAMERA IS ROLLING

Our video camera is rolling,
Recording our lives for the next generations to see.
Our simple wedding,
Our children's healthy births,
Every Merry Christmas,
Every Happy New Year,
All our fun friends,
Families over here and over there.

Our video camera is rolling,
Recording our lives to watch when we're old,
Working in our garden,
Picking apples,
Painting the house,
Decorating our home,
Singing love songs in duet.

Our video camera is rolling,
Storing the good life we have,
Playing music,
Dancing with the children,
Kicking a soccer ball,
Building a snowman,
Swimming with the neighbors.

Our video camera is rolling,
Capturing the family we have.
Everything is recorded,
Even our unspoken dreams,
For the next generations to see.

PART TWO: Endings, Grief, And Loss

*Take away love
and our earth is a tomb.*

Robert Browning

THE FIRE NO MORE

We were everything we wanted to be here:
Believers and sinners,
Takers and givers,
Strangers who fell in love,
Lovers who could love no more.

We dreamed of everything here:
Distant places,
Close relationships,
Walks hand in hand,
But we could hold them no more.

We experienced everything here:
Native words,
Foreign accents,
Exotic feelings
That we could sense no more.

We saw everything here,
But not what was coming:
The end of our roads,
And walks,
And love in our hearts.

*We must let go of the life we have planned,
so as to accept the one that is waiting for us.*

Joseph Campbell

GOODBYE, OUR HOME

*E*very step I took around our yard,
Before we went our separate ways,
Took me back in time.

I saw you picking cucumbers from the garden
And hauling them home in an old toy wagon.
I saw our girls playing ball on the grass by the pool.
Heard their voices echo in the woods.
I saw myself push them higher than the stars, higher than the moon
On the tallest swing in the neighborhood.

I turned my head toward a familiar sound coming from our patio
And saw you cleaning rugs, beating them against the house.

Later, before bedtime, I saw you waving from the living room window
While holding first a naked Monika,
And years later a naked Ania, before their baths.

Then I saw the glass of lemonade you brought to me at dusk.
I can still taste it.
Oh, yes—I can still taste those days.

With my eyes too wet for me to see,
With my heart too heavy for me to walk,
I sat on a stone and cried,
And everything around cried with me.
You locked the house, sat next to me,
And we cried for the first and last time together.

*We are healed of a suffering
only by expressing it to the full.*

Marcel Proust

THE LAST RIDE TO OUR HOUSE

The ride to our house, that soon will become someone else's home,
Was too short.
With the music written just for the occasion,
With the sun at the right angle for this moment,
I could drive endlessly toward our house.
No stops, no intersections, no problems,
Just the two of us in the car filled with tunes and the freedom to feel.

I still tried to hide my tears,
But those days of never letting them out are gone now.
I still tried to talk wisely,
But those times of having all the answers are also gone.

A grasp of mistakes, the honesty of speech, and the simplicity of action
Have begun building their nests in me.
And I like that.
I feel relieved from false obligation to find manipulative words
In order to accomplish yet another of my goals,
To construct my flawed kingdom,
To build my fake paradise ruled by self-defined commandments,
To dig my own spiritual grave, eventually.

Later, slightly touching one another,
We lay on the floor of our old living room.
I glared at the ceiling but, this time, could not see any images in it.
All mirages are gone.
All furnishings are gone.
Our home is gone, too.
But we still live and breathe, in spite of everything.
And tomorrow we will start dreaming again.
We'll take a step into the future,
And then another, and then one more.
We'll try to choose between what's just and what's pleasant,
What's forever and what's for now.
We'll try to find the road that ends
In the neighborhood with no houses for sale for the wrong reasons,
With no empty living rooms,
With no children saying, "I want to go home, Dad!"

Hope is like a road in the country:
there was never a road,
but when many people walk on it,
the road comes into existence.

Lin Yutang

THERE ARE DAYS THESE DAYS

There are days these days
When I can almost breathe, almost function,
Almost smile, and almost peek into the future again.
There are days these days
When I can almost see past my children's pain,
Past my mother's shattered heart,
Past my brothers' and sisters' "Whys?"

There are days these days
When I can almost see myself full of life again,
Running in the woods,
Fishing way past sunset,
Rolling in the grass,
Planting another forest in my new yard.

There are days these days
When I begin to recognize
The little boy I abandoned,
My faulty desires,
My spinelessness,
My fear of being alone.

He cried.
I ignored him.

On days like these, I aspire
To dig him out from underneath my life's ruins,
To take him for a walk...
Hand in hand,
Heart in heart,
The man and the boy,
To sing together, "Never again, my friend. Never again!"

*To a father growing old
nothing is dearer than a daughter.*

Euripides

DAUGHTER'S THOUGHTS

I am young.
I am silly.
I don't know yet what's wrong and what's not,
But when I look into my life's eyes
I see the tears my grandmothers cried,
I remember the tears my mother shed,
I hear the ones my father swallowed.

And later, I feel my sister hugging me,
Comforting me,
Talking to me as if she were my mother.

But what do people see in my eight-year-old face?
Do they see that someday I will,
Just like all women do,
Smile and cry,
Dance and mourn,
Give and take.
But most of all,
I will always be like them,
Like my dad and like my mom
Because I am what they are,
Two imperfect people
Who tried their best.

A confession
has to be part of your new life.

Ludwig Wittgenstein

I WASH MY CAR

*I*n my communal, heated garage,
I frequently wash my car this winter.
I do it by myself.
Manually.
With a hose, dish soap, and a towel.

I take time to wash my car this winter.
I spray it first with water.
I wait.
I soak it and let the soap fight the dirt.

I find pleasure in washing my car this winter.
It amuses me to watch it becoming so clean, so quickly.
Right in front of my eyes,
In a few blinks,
The work of my hands
Turns filth into purity,
Dust into clarity,
And sends dirt down the floor drain to vanish forever.

Why can't I change so quickly?
Why can't I become pure in a matter of minutes?
Why can't I pour my contaminated-with-sins blood down the drain?
Why can't I be like my car during this never-ending winter?

I keep on washing my car in my communal, heated garage this winter,
And keep on thinking about the dirt in me.
About the goodnight kisses I did not lay.
The flowers I did not bring.
The poems I did not write.
The "I love yous" I did not whisper.
The love I did not uphold.
The signs I did not read.
The family I did not save.
The life I let derail.

PART THREE: Finding Love Again

*There is only one happiness in life,
to love and be loved.*

George Sand

DISCOVERING YOU

*L*ike a magic eye, I hope to perceive you
Hidden in a vibrant picture made of life's illusions
Where colors of love, trust, and happiness
Compose its three-dimensional image.

With an attentive ear, I hope to hear your heart beat.
A heart petrified from giving "No!" for an answer,
Longing for unconditional love,
Divided into pieces like Jesus's bread,
Misread as insufficient but able to feed all.

With perceptive eyes, I hope to discover
A new smile on your lips,
A new movement of your hands,
A new grimace on your face,
A new style of your hair,
New pajamas you put on,
A new wrinkle you camouflage from view,
And an uninvited gray hair on your head.

I hope to discover something new in you forever.

And even if you claim you did nothing unusual on a particular day,
Even if you swear you are the same as you were yesterday,
I will find a new footprint behind you in a new place,
See a flower that you've touched while walking through the garden,
Or at night, with my fingers and my lips,
Learn a new detail of your body.

And when I'm old,
With trembling hands, but cloudless consciousness,
I hope to complete my search and say,
"I found you."

*And the day came
when the risk it took to stay tight in the bud
was more than the risk it took to blossom.*

Anaïs Nin

CAN WE? CAN I? CAN YOU?

Can we hear the music, girl?
The music around us,
Between our heavy breaths,
Between our lips?

Can I say the truth, girl?
The truth about my earnest fears,
The fear of loneliness,
The fear of being incapable of loving again?

Can you feel the hands, girl?
My hands around you,
Between your words,
Between our past and our future?

Standing on the edge of a new beginning,
Looking into it with trepidation and anticipation,
Can we honestly say that NOW we know
What went wrong?
What went right?
What's gone and is never coming back?
That this time will be better?
That this time we'll love harder?
That this time will be THE ONLY TIME?

Can we? Can I? Can you?

*At the touch of love
everyone becomes a poet.*

Plato

I WILL BE YOUR AIR

*T*here is no better gift to meadows and flowers
Than to be watered by early spring showers.
There is no better feeling to a drop of rain
Than to hear the other drops' splashing refrain.

There is no better sound to sleepy trees
Than to hear the wind's serene breeze.
There is no better hope to a love-starved soul
Than to find someone precious, to feel whole.

I am giving you my heart. Can you give me yours?
Let's give us each other, let love open all doors.
If I cry in your arms, will you cry with me?
If you cross the river, I will cross the sea.

There is no better road, no better endeavor
Than the one for better, for worse, forever.
You are in me now. You're my soul, my prayer.
For as long as you breathe, I will be your air.

Reflection

Part One: Coming To America

*R*efugees went through basic training about life in America before leaving Austria, but nothing could prepare us fully for the beauty, the amazing people, or the complications awaiting us. The greatest obstacle was the lack of language skills. I came to America not knowing the English language at all.

The help I received when I arrived made a world of difference in my young American life. There was no one in Clarion, Iowa, who spoke Polish, so my communication with everybody from the First Lutheran Church, which formed the sponsoring committee, was rough at first. But those wonderful people paid for my airplane ticket, my rent, my food, and my basic needs, until I found a job several weeks later.

Facing a new culture, traditions, language, and homesickness created many challenges for me. Still, I was excited to be here, and I dove into my American life with full force and enthusiasm.

I married an American woman from Iowa in 1987. Shortly after that, we moved to Minneapolis, Minnesota, where we found jobs. I was trying to follow my dream of becoming a rock star at the time. (I let that dream go after I recorded myself singing for the first time.) Our first daughter, Monika, was born in 1989. In 1993, my wife and I managed to build a beautiful home. Soon after, our second daughter, Ania, was born. Life was busy, but good.

Part Two: Endings, Grief, and Loss

After sixteen years, our marriage fell apart. Saying goodbye to everything we worked so hard to create was difficult, and looking into my children's eyes in those days was heartbreaking, as was reading the divorce decree. I struggled to accept the reality of being unable to see my kids every day.

With passing time, helpful books, and the support of people who listened to me, I started to come to grips with reality. I realized I needed to move on, to believe in a better future. Our kids would be okay, and I would, too.

Admitting to my faults was a major part of my recovery. I felt, and still feel, guilty for letting this happen to my marriage and to my children.

Part Three: Finding Love Again

It took about three years after the divorce for me to feel like a normal man. Thinking about love and relationships started to feel good again.

Today, I spend as much time as I can with my children. In recent years, we traveled together to Europe several times to visit my family. For the second time in my American life I am rebuilding my life, but this time I am doing it on my own.

CHAPTER V

Now

*There is always one moment
in childhood when the door opens
and lets the future in.*

Deepak Chopra

I STILL HEAR

I still hear the sound of the gate to our family's yard,
Its soft thump
Echoing in the orchard,
The swish of my bare feet on the sandy path home.

I still hear the rattle of our family's hand water pump,
Its iron struggles,
Every rasp,
Every spout in the bucket.

I still hear each creak and groan of our family's sofa,
Its nightly listening
To our family prayers,
Our kneeling in humility.

I still hear the simplicity that I used to be ashamed of.
And today,
I am ashamed
Of feeling ashamed then.

Death is not the greatest loss in life. The greatest loss is what dies inside us while we live.

Norman Cousins

THE RIVER

There was only one river in our village,
A place for people to dump garbage,
For cows to urinate,
Dead water carrying dead objects,
Including my father.

He left home early one morning, late one fall,
And he never returned.

For forty bone- and heart-chilling days and nights, we waited.
We cried on each side of the telephone line
And prayed on each side of the ocean.

My brothers searched the village.
My sisters walked the woods and meadows.
They followed every noise and every shadow.

But he was nowhere.

We prayed again.
Prayed more.
Prayed harder.
Prayed in two different languages,
On two different continents,
But prayed to one Almighty.
For help, we prayed!

My brothers searched each house and barn,
My sisters went around each stack of hay,
They stopped at all crossroads and every dead end.

But they never checked the river,
A place where people dump their garbage,
Where cows urinate,
Where my father's body soaked for forty days,
Waiting for us to find it.

Dance as if no one were watching,
Sing as if no one were listening,
And live every day as if it were your last.

Irish Proverb

YOUR FIRST DANCE

I feel, for the first time, that you are not my child anymore.
Here I am, standing next to you, looking at you, admiring you,
But also feeling separated like a tree from its fallen apple.

Things will never be the same between us.
No more telling you what to do or how to do it.
No more singing goodnight songs or praying together at your bedside.

I feel like I am losing you,
Losing you forever.
And now, I fear I may not have done enough to let you fly on your own,
Or that I may not have been the best father I could have been to you.
Was I enough of a mentor and friend to prepare you for what's ahead?
For your own decision-making?
For your own life-making?
For your own understanding of our world,
Your world,
The world of your children, and their children,
All children starting with you?
Was I wise enough to make you wise?
Was I loving enough so you know what unconditional love is?
So you can love yourself,
Love others, love love even if it breaks your heart?

If I could go back in time, child,
I'd make you better, stronger, softer.
I'd show you more sunsets and more sunrises.
I'd teach you to hear the songs of the falling leaves in the aging forest.
I'd touch your hands more often,
So you would remember my skin,
My heart, my gray hair, my accent, my guilt,
My love that was too often buried under the excuses of my frantic life.

Dance, girl, dance!
You are eighteen only once!

Love the whole world
as a mother loves her only child.

Buddha

RETURN

*M*y first time going back to Poland,
After leaving it for what I thought would be forever,
Was a surprise visit.

I opened the gate to my family yard.
The smell of flowers,
The sense of home,
The bliss of unexpected returns.
Just as I imagined.

Through the leaves of an apple tree
I saw my mom sitting on the front step,
Peeling potatoes for her lonely dinner.
She paused as if she could hear me hiding.
Tears pushed through her eyes,
Ran down her wrinkled face,
And splashed on the bottom of the potato bucket.

I dove through flowers and gooseberry bushes.
Through an unbearable past
And years of separation.
Through her grief
And my pain.

"Mama!"

Breathless.
Speechless.

Her arms around me.
My head on her shoulder.
Our hearts intertwined.
Sobbing.

"I knew it," she whispered.
"I knew I would hold you again."

*For everything
there is a season
...a time to weep,
and a time to laugh.*

Ecclesiastes 3:1-8

IN US

*F*or every ending,
	there is a start.
For each tear that falls,
	there is a broken heart.
For each passing moment,
	there is a speck of dust.
For each wary person,
	there are people who trust.
For each step we take,
	there is a print in the sand.
For each deep wish,
	there is a shallow command.
For each narrow path,
	there is an open field.
For each unguarded chest,
	there is a shield.
For every nightmare,
	there is a quiet dream.
For every whisper,
	there is a scream.
For every river,
	there is a dam.
For every woman,
	there is a man.
For each new start,
	there must be an end.
For each honest man,
	there are men who pretend.
For each word of wisdom,
	there is a deed of shame.
We are all different.
	We are all the same.

*How we spend
our days is, of course,
how we spend our lives.*

Annie Dillard

NOT ENOUGH TIME

I had a late start to my American life.
At forty-two, I finished college.
At forty-seven, I discovered my path.
I am years behind, but I take this road.

I live here as if there were no end to my life.
I plan the future as if I have centuries to spare.
My wrinkled face pays the price of passing time,
But my dreams don't age—they never rest.

I walk as if all my roads have happy endings.
I sleep without fear of not waking up.
But will there be enough time in my American life
To feel at home here, to improve, to understand?

Sometimes, I stop my march to catch my breath,
To assess what's left to do and what must be done.
But then I run—run into the future,
Faster and faster with each step, each day.

At night, only the force of eyelid-shutting darkness
Drags my tired feet to my unmade bed.
I don't want to sleep—it's a waste of time!
I need to sprint, to work, to create!

In bed, I pray for my children's future,
For letting them live the way I knew I could,
For enough days to see them fly,
Enough nights to see them land.

In the morning, as always now, I run into living.
Like an icebreaker, I push through the crowds.
Crowds of my needs,
Of my desires,
Of my restless American life.

Make the most of yourself,
for that is all there is of you.

Ralph Waldo Emerson

THE FEAR I FEAR

*I*n my old world,
A world of lies, propaganda, and a fear of police,
They trained us to be scared.

In my old world,
A world of drunken citizens,
Smoke-filled houses and schools,
Restrooms with no toilet paper,
My scared heart crushed my ribs.
They trained me well to fear.

But now,
I don't fear police sirens,
Opening doors,
Praying with children.
I am not scared to say
What I like,
What I don't,
What I did,
What is wrong.

I don't even fear getting older,
Nor that death will come one day.

The only fear I fear here,
Is that while alive,
I don't live completely enough.

To succeed,
we must first believe that we can.

Michael Korda

I MUST BELIEVE

I believe all things are possible,
That one can change his fate,
Wildest rivers can be crossed,
Highest mountains climbed,
Every grain of sand counted,
Every child fed.

I believe we waste lives fighting battles,
And we often lose our wars.
I believe in ordinary heroes
Who die for extraordinary reasons,
Reasons we too quickly forget.

I believe in straightforwardness of questions,
That habits can be changed.
I believe that greed is shameless
And compassion limitless.
I believe love is a gift,
And a gift is love.

I believe we can be blinded.
I believe we can see.
I believe in our wisdom.
I believe.
I must believe.

*Contentment is not the
fulfillment of what you want,
but the realization
of how much you already have.*

Unknown

MY MIRROR FOR LIFE

With a big splash
I drop my lake between two American valleys.
It fits like friends' hands in an honest shake.
I wait until the surface calms,
Until it is perfectly smooth and clear,
Like a mirror.

With goose bumps all over my body
I look into it.
I see myself clearly like never before.
I see my talents,
My strengths,
My desires float to the surface.

With hands shaped into a bowl, I scoop them out
And toss them high in the air, over my head.
They mingle,
Rejoice,
Turn,
Fall,
Cover my face,
My body,
The rest of my life.

Soak me!
Stay with me!
Be my mirror for life.

*I am not afraid of tomorrow,
for I have seen yesterday
and I love today.*

William Allen White

I'D DO IT ALL AGAIN

*I*t's been more than twenty years since I came to America.
More than two decades of a life so different from what I had.
A life of new faces,
New voices,
New passions,
New challenges,
New aspirations.

There were years when I fell in love
With new toys,
New heroes,
New lessons,
New religions,
New possibilities.

There were years of building
New houses,
New homes,
New yards,
New neighborhoods,
New visions.

Years of struggles
With homesickness,
Divorce,
Heartbroken children,
Our parents,
Deaths.

But the years that matter most
Are those still ahead.
Years of growth,
Of giving back,
Of simplification,
Of my children living in peace,
Of all children living in peace.

And for those years I'd do it all again.

Reflection

I can't look into the future without remembering the past. My history, no matter how unpleasant it sometimes was, keeps me in check when my mind becomes greedy, or when I start feeling sorry for myself. In such moments, I recall my grandfather who died in Auschwitz, my grandmother who spent years in prison during the war, the difficult life my mother had, and the dead-end streets I walked during those days of communism in Poland. These memories help me to appreciate what I have, what I can still accomplish, and what a great opportunity the next generation of Raginiaks has in America.

I am now able to help my family back in Poland, and I can show my children the world. They can grow up as global citizens with a global understanding of issues. And, of course, if I hadn't come to America, I would not have had these children—and I can't imagine my life without them.

Final Reflection

I share these poems and reflections to encourage others to embrace the power of their potential, so they can find their path in life and escape to their freedom. Once I arrived in America, I had new things to learn about what it means to be free. I realized that there is no limit to what is possible.

I hope you will write your own poems. To help you with that, on my website, I have placed EXERCISES that correspond with each chapter of the book. They are free and ready for your book club or personal discovery and journey into your soul. Please find them at www.1moment.us/myescapetofreedom.htm.

Every step of my journey brought me closer to the understanding of how deeply each person impacts the lives of others. I'd like to hear your discoveries, insights, and ideas for future books and programs. Please email me at chez@1moment.us.

For more information on my presentations and programs, visit my web site at www.1moment.us.

Chez Raginiak